Favourite

BOATING

Compiled by Ca

~ TERRY WHITWORTH ~

SALMON

Index

Cover pictures: *front:* Cropredy Lock, Oxford Canal
back: Autumn Sunrise on the Cut. From paintings by Alan Firth

Printed and published by Dorrigo, Manchester, England © Copyright

Pork and Apricot Casserole

Preserving fruit and vegetables is an ancient process; the Romans are known to have pickled an astonishing assortment including lemons, plums, peaches and apricots. It is a good idea always to keep a supply of dried fruits, pickles and chutneys on board.

1 lb pork fillet	**1 tablespoon tomato purée**
Seasoned flour	**¾ pint vegetable stock**
8 button onions or shallots, chopped	**3 oz dried apricots**
1 clove garlic, finely chopped	**1 teaspoon dried mixed herbs**
4 oz mushrooms, sliced	**Salt and pepper**
	Oil for frying

Set oven to 325°F or Mark 3. Season the flour and place in a large plastic bag. Thickly slice the pork, put it into the flour bag and shake well to coat evenly. This is a useful tip for working in the confined space of a small galley; it also saves washing up. Heat 2 tablespoons of oil in a large, flameproof casserole and fry the onions and mushrooms until they are golden. Add the pork and chopped garlic and fry for a few moments, then lower the heat, add the tomato purée, stock and any remaining flour and stir. Add the apricots and mixed herbs and season well. Stir again, bring to the boil, cover, put in the oven and cook for 1½ hours or until the meat is tender. Serve with mashed potatoes, boiled rice or couscous. Serves 4.

DOLLY

Alan firth

Gooseberry and Almond Pudding

Boat people often had to snatch meals between working locks, steering and generally keeping their world on the move. A hot meal with a substantial pudding was, therefore, a welcome end to a long and tiring day.

6 oz gooseberries	**2 eggs**
4 oz shredded suet	**¼ pint milk**
4 oz fresh breadcrumbs	**1 oz ground almonds**
4 oz soft brown sugar	**3-4 drops almond essence**
(or more if preferred)	**Pinch of salt**

Top and tail and wash the gooseberries. Cut them in half and put in a mixing bowl with the suet, breadcrumbs, sugar and a pinch of salt. Beat the eggs in a separate bowl with the ground almonds and almond essence and stir in the milk. Stir the liquid slowly into the dry ingredients; the mixture should have a soft, dropping consistency. Leave to stand for 15 minutes. Well grease a 2 pint pudding basin, put the mixture into it, cover with kitchen foil and seal. Steam for 45 minutes to 1 hour until firm, topping up the water if necessary. Serve with custard. Serves 6.

Sausage Casserole

Thick, meaty pork sausages from a good butcher are best for this dish.
Try using spicy flavoured sausages for variety.

2 lbs pork sausages	**1 teaspoon mixed herbs**
1 medium onion, chopped	**1 teaspoon sugar**
2 cloves garlic, chopped	**Salt and pepper**
14 oz tin of tomatoes,	**1 dessertspoon cornflour**
roughly chopped	**½ pt vegetable stock**
1 tablespoon tomato purée	**2 cups frozen peas**

Oil for frying

Cut the sausages in half. Heat 1 tablespoon of oil in a large saucepan and fry the sausages slowly, until browned. Remove and set aside. Add another tablespoon of oil and fry the onion and garlic until soft but not brown. Replace the sausages and add the chopped tomatoes, tomato purée, herbs and sugar and stir. Mix the cornflour with a tablespoon of stock in a bowl then stir in the remainder of the stock and mix well. Add to the casserole, stir and season well. Bring to the boil, cover and simmer for 35 to 40 minutes, adding more boiling water if required during cooking. Add the peas 5 minutes before the end of the cooking time. Serves 4-6.

Turkey Tardebigge

On the Worcester and Birmingham Canal the Tardebigge flight of thirty locks coupled with the six at Stoke make a total of thirty-six locks in four miles. A crew completing this mammoth task needs a good meal and a well-earned rest. This tasty dish is simple to prepare; just the thing for such an occasion.

4-6 turkey breasts, cut into slices	**2 tablespoons mango chutney**
1 tablespoon butter	**2 tablespoons tomato purée**
1 tablespoon oil	**2 tablespoons medium curry paste**
2 medium onions, chopped	**Water**
3 cloves garlic, crushed	**Salt**

Crush the garlic with a good pinch of salt. Heat the butter and oil in a large saucepan and fry the onions gently until soft but not brown. Add the garlic. Remove from the heat, put the slices of turkey breasts in the pan, add the chutney, tomato purée and curry paste and stir well. Slowly pour on enough water to cover all the ingredients and check the salt. Bring to the boil, cover, lower the heat and simmer for 40-45 minutes until the turkey is tender, stirring occasionally to prevent sticking. Add more boiling water if necessary. Serve with a green salad and crusty bread. Serves 4 to 6.

Seven

Windfall Apple Pudding

There is something satisfying about gathering up windfall apples. In the old days nothing was ever wasted and it is easy to imagine a boat wife walking along the towpath, perhaps with the horse or going ahead to set a lock, finding fallen apples and putting them in her pocket.

PASTRY

6 oz flour   **3 oz cooking fats**   **Pinch of salt**   **Cold water to mix**

FILLING

2 large eating apples   **1 large cooking apple**   **2 oz seedless raisins,**
1 egg   **2 oz caster sugar**   **1 oz self raising flour**   **Icing sugar for dredging**

Set over to 375°F or Mark 5. **Pastry**. Put the fats, salt and flour into a bowl, cut the fat into small pieces and rub in lightly. Add about 1½ tablespoons water and mix with a fork. Knead lightly and roll out on a floured surface and line an 8 inch pie plate. Overlap the rim by ½ inch and turn back the pastry overlap to form a double rim. **Filling**. Peel, core and slice the apples, mix with the raisins and pile in the pastry case. Beat the egg and sugar together in a bowl until thick and creamy, fold in the flour and pour over the filling. Bake for 35 minutes or until golden brown. Dredge with icing sugar and serve with custard or pouring cream. Serves 4.

Lift-up bridge near Wrenbury, Llangollen Canal

Lock-keeper's Onion Soup

Many lock-keepers have beautifully kept and productive gardens beside their cottages, growing both flowers and vegetables. This full-bodied soup was inspired by some really giant, prize-winning onions bought from one such lock-side garden.

4 large onions, finely chopped   **1 ¾ pints vegetable stock**
1 tablespoon oil for frying   **1 teaspoon yeast extract**
Black pepper

Heat the oil in a large saucepan and fry the onions gently until just softened. Add the stock and the yeast extract and stir well. Season with plenty of freshly ground black pepper. Bring to the boil, stirring, then cover and simmer gently until the onions are really soft. Serve with large chunks of crusty bread. Serves 6 to 8.

Baked Fish Pie

There is something exciting about arriving by boat at an unknown town; shops to explore and markets to wander around. This dish uses a mixture of smoked and un-smoked fish.

1 ¾ lbs cod fillet and smoked haddock, about half each
3 lbs potatoes   1 pint milk   2 oz butter   1 bay leaf
1 tablespoon chopped fresh parsley   2 oz flour

Set oven to 375°F or Mark 5. Boil the potatoes and mash with 3 tablespoons of milk taken from the pint and a knob of butter, cover and set aside. Wash the fish and put into a saucepan with the remaining milk and the bay leaf. Bring to the boil then simmer for 10-15 minutes. When cooked, drain off the milk and bay leaf and set aside. Next flake the fish, removing all skin and bones. Butter an ovenproof dish and spread the fish over the bottom, add the chopped parsley and season well. Melt the butter in a pan, remove from the heat, stir in the flour and beat well. Slowly add the milk (remove the bay leaf) mixing well and beat again. Return to the heat, stirring continually until the sauce boils and thickens. Pour over the fish and then cover with the mashed potatoes and rough up with a fork. Put the dish on a baking sheet or on kitchen foil in the oven in case it bubbles over and cook until it is heated through and the potato nicely browned on top. Serves 4.

Boiled Beef and Carrots

This dish has stood the test of time and is an old favourite. It is straightforward to cook, gives a good hot meal on one day and provides cold meat on the next. This is a valuable attribute when planning meals for a hungry boat crew.

2-3 lbs topside or **8-10 medium carrots, sliced**
silverside of beef **1 small swede, thickly sliced**
2 oz butter **1-2 teaspoons dried herbs**
2 large onions, sliced **½-¾ pint vegetable stock**
Salt and pepper

First ensure the meat is securely tied. Melt the butter in a large flameproof casserole and brown the meat all over. Remove and set aside. Next lightly fry the onions, then add the swede and carrots and continue until just beginning to brown. Replace the meat in the dish on the bed of vegetables. Sprinkle over the dried herbs, season well and pour on the stock. Bring to the boil, cover and cook in the oven for 1-1½ hours until the meat is tender. Alternatively simmer on top of the stove for about 2 hours. Serve with mashed potatoes. Serves 4 to 6.

Salmon in the Pot

In times gone by, salmon was an inexpensive fish readily available to most people, including boaters, especially if they were working near to a river like the Severn.

4 salmon steaks	**6 peppercorns**
1 small onion, sliced	**4 tablespoons vinegar**
1 small carrot, cut into thin strips	**2 teaspoons lemon juice**
6-8 slices cucumber	**Pinch of salt**

Put the onion, carrot, cucumber and peppercorns into a large saucepan or flameproof casserole. Lay the salmon steaks on top of the vegetables, add the vinegar and just enough water to cover the fish, and season. Bring to the boil, cover and boil for 3 minutes then remove from the heat immediately. Carefully lift the salmon steaks from the pan, place in a dish and strain over the hot liquid together with the lemon juice. Cover and allow to cool. When cold, transfer each salmon steak on to an individual bed of crispy lettuce and surround with spoonfuls of the vegetable mixture. Serves 4.

Courgette and Lentil Bake

Courgettes are used in this dish, but a young marrow is equally suitable. Traditionally, working narrow boats were painted with colourful designs of stylised roses and castles. These still persist on today's pleasure craft and have been joined by fruit and even the occasional vegetable.

8 oz red split lentils (no soak)	**4 courgettes or 1 young marrow**
1 medium onion, chopped	**2 cloves garlic, finely chopped**
1 oz butter	**1 tablespoon oil**
2 teaspoons curry paste	**Salt and pepper**

Put the lentils into a saucepan, cover with water and add the chopped onion. Bring to the boil and simmer until the lentils are soft, then drain off any surplus water. Add the butter and curry paste, stir well and set aside in the pan. Wash the courgettes and cut into slices; if using a marrow, peel and cut into chunks. Chop the garlic finely. Heat the oil in a frying pan and toss the courgettes or marrow, browning slightly over a high heat. Lower the heat and add the lentil mixture with the garlic and stir. Cover and cook gently over a low heat for about 10 minutes. Serve with boiled rice and a green salad. Serves 4 to 6.

Lock-Keeper's Casserole

Lock-keepers' local knowledge is invaluable and they can offer words of encouragement, information about canal and weather conditions or directions to the nearest shop or pub.

4-6 joints of rabbit	**8 oz mushrooms sliced**
Seasoned flour	**8 oz streaky bacon, de-rinded**
2 oz butter	**and cut into 1 inch pieces**
2 medium onions, chopped	**½ pint vegetable stock**
2 medium carrots, sliced	**2 teaspoons tomato purée**
2 medium apples, peeled,	**Sprig of fresh thyme or**
cored and thickly sliced	**1 teaspoon dried thyme**

Salt and pepper

Heat half the butter in a large saucepan and cook the onions, carrots and apples for 5 minutes, stirring well. Remove from the pan and set aside. Coat the rabbit joints in seasoned flour. Heat the remaining butter in the pan and brown the rabbit joints on both sides. Lower the heat, add the mushrooms and bacon pieces and continue cooking for 5 minutes. Add the stock slowly and then add the apple/vegetable mixture, the tomato purée and thyme, stirring all the time, and season. Bring to the boil, cover, lower the heat and simmer for 1 hour or until the rabbit is tender. Stir occasionally and add more stock or boiling water if required. Serves 4 to 6.

At Stoke Bruerne, Grand Union Canal

Alan Firth

Potato Layer Bake

This dish can be a meal on its own or it can be used to accompany hot or cold meat.
Although the preparation takes a little time the result is well worth the effort and,
once in the oven, it more or less looks after itself.

4-6 large potatoes, sliced	**3 cloves garlic, chopped**
1-1½ pints milk	**1 oz butter**
2 large onions, chopped	**Salt and pepper**

Set oven to 375°F or Mark 5. Well butter a large, ovenproof dish. Crush the garlic with a good pinch of salt. Peel the potatoes, wash and pat dry and cut into fairly thin slices. Place a layer of potatoes in the bottom of the dish and sprinkle over a layer of garlic and onion. Season well with black pepper and a little more salt if preferred. Continue in layers, finishing with a layer of potatoes. Pour the milk over and dot with butter. Cover with kitchen foil and cook for about 1 hour, removing the covering about 10 minutes before the end of the cooking time to brown the top. Serves 4 to 6.

Fried Eels

Eels abound in many canals and rivers and can be caught by rod and line, though commercially, special traps are used. They also migrate across damp, dewy fields in the moonlight in order to reach isolated ponds.

2 lbs eels	**Seasoned flour**
1 egg, beaten	**1 oz butter**

Wash and skin the eels and cut into chunks about 2 inches thick. Coat with beaten egg and then dust in the seasoned flour. Melt the butter in a large frying pan until it is really hot and sizzling. Fry the eels, very gently, turning once just to seal them; it is important not to brown them or they will over cook. Then turn down the heat, cover the pan and continue cooking, covered, until the flesh is tender. As eels can be rather oily, fresh crusty bread goes well with this dish. Serves 4.

Damson, Cinnamon and Apple Pudding

Damson trees are a wonderful sight in Spring with their clouds of white blossom and in Autumn there is the bounty of their downy, purple fruits. Mixing damsons and cinnamon together with apples makes a delicious autumn pudding.

½ lb damsons	2 egg yolks
½ lb cooking apples	4 tablespoons fresh white breadcrumbs
2 oz butter, unsalted	½ pint double cream
4 oz sugar (or more if preferred)	1 teaspoon ground cinnamon

Wash the damsons and peel, core and thinly slice the apples. Melt the butter in a saucepan, add the fruit and sugar, just cover with water and simmer until the fruit is soft. When cooked, cool and purée the fruit, remove the stones and add more sugar if preferred. Blend in the egg yolks and the breadcrumbs. Stir the mixture over a low heat until thickened then put into a bowl and leave to cool. Meanwhile, whisk the cream lightly and then fold in to the cooled fruit purée, add the cinnamon and mix well. When cold, spoon into individual bowls or sundae glasses and serve. Serves 4.

Mixed Mushroom Compote

In autumn the canal-side fields and woods can yield a delectable harvest of edible mushrooms. However, for those who are inexperienced in identification, a mixture bought from a reliable source is a safer solution.

8-12 oz mixed mushrooms, sliced   **2 oz butter**
2 cloves garlic, crushed   **1 teaspoon dried mixed herbs**
1 medium onion, finely chopped   **Salt and pepper**

Wipe and slice the mushrooms, crush the garlic with a pinch of salt and finely chop the onion. Heat the butter in a saucepan over a moderate heat and cook the onions, without browning, stirring constantly. Add the garlic paste, the mushrooms and the dried herbs, season and stir again. Lower the heat, cover the pan and cook for 5 minutes. Remove the lid and, stirring well, turn up the heat and boil until the liquid has reduced somewhat and has browned slightly. Serve at once on hot buttered toast. Serves 4 to 6.

Rhubarb and Ginger Flan

Plant pots and containers sit happily on cabin roofs and outside cabin doors.
Flowers and herbs grow well in these conditions and even rhubarb can be
forced in a bucket to give an early crop.

6 oz shortcrust pastry	**2 level tablespoons flour**
1 lb rhubarb	**1 teaspoon ground ginger**
2 oz caster sugar (or more if preferred)	**¼ pint double cream**

Set oven to 425°F or Mark 7. Roll out the pastry on a lightly floured surface to ⅛ inch thick, line an 8 inch flan ring and set aside in a cool place. Cut off the leaves and white ends from the rhubarb sticks. Wash the sticks well, dry, slice diagonally into ½ inch pieces and arrange evenly over the pastry case. Whisk together in a bowl the sugar, flour, ground ginger and cream and spoon the mixture over the rhubarb. Bake for 30 minutes or until the pastry is golden. Serve hot or cold. If eating hot, allow to cool slightly or it will be difficult to serve. Serves 6.

Steak and Kidney Pudding

The main feature of a working narrowboat cabin was the coal-fired range, the boat wife's pride and joy. Not only did she look after the children and cook, wash, clean and shop for the family but she also steered the boat when on the move.

2 lbs chuck steak, diced   8 oz ox kidney, diced   1 medium onion, chopped
1 teaspoon chopped parsley   ¼ pint water   Salt and pepper
PASTRY
1 lb flour   6 oz shredded suet   Pinch of salt   Cold water

Pastry: Sift together the flour and salt in a bowl and add the suet. Mix well, carefully adding sufficient water, a little at a time, to produce a firm dough; too wet and it will not roll out property. Roll out on a lightly floured surface sufficient to line a 2 pint pudding basin and make a lid. Line the basin, leaving the overhanging pastry. **Filling.** Put layers of steak and kidney, onion, parsley and seasoning successively into the basin until near the top then pour in the water. Wet the pastry edges, put on the lid, turn back the overhang and seal the edge well. Cover and seal with kitchen foil. Put into a large saucepan, fill with water to about three quarters of the depth of the basin, bring to the boil, cover and simmer briskly for 3-4 hours. Top up with boiling water as necessary. To serve, wrap a clean napkin around and serve straight from the basin. Serves 4 to 6.

Winkwell Watercress Soup

In days gone by fresh watercress could be obtained directly from clear flowing brooks in the countryside, as well as from managed watercress beds like those beside the Grand Union Canal at Winkwell. Nowadays, owing to possible pollution, it is probably wiser to buy professionally grown bunches.

2 bunches fresh watercress	**2 oz butter**
1 lb potatoes, thickly sliced	**1 bay leaf**
2 large onions, chopped	**Salt and pepper**
2 pints vegetable stock	**3-4 tablespoons milk**

Wash the watercress well. Put the watercress, potato slices, onions, stock and butter into a large saucepan with the bay leaf and season well. Bring to the boil, cover and then simmer until the potatoes and onions are soft. Remove the bay leaf and rub the soup through a sieve into a clean saucepan, add the milk, stir well, adjust the seasoning and reheat, but do not boil. Serves 6 to 8.

Barney Boat Stew

Many pleasure boats on Britain's inland waterways are based on old, working narrowboats and are beautifully painted with roses and castles. Among these are the class known as 'Barney' boats with charming names as 'Watershrimp', 'Cushie Butterfield' and 'Rambling Rose'.

2 lbs. lean pork	8 oz. mushrooms, sliced
Seasoned flour	2 sticks celery, medium sliced
1 pint vegetable stock	1 red or yellow pepper, de-seeded and
½ - 1½ teaspoons yeast extract	cut into strips
2 large onions, chopped	2 teaspoons mixed dried herbs
1 large parsnip, diced	Oil for frying
1 large leek, thinly sliced	Salt and pepper

Cut the meat into 1 inch cubes and toss in seasoned flour. Put 2 tablespoons of oil in a large pan and fry the meat until browned all over. Reduce the heat and add the stock and yeast extract and stir. Bring to the boil, cover and set to simmer over a low heat. Meanwhile gently fry the onions in a tablespoon of oil until soft but not brown and then add to the meat with all the other prepared vegetables and the herbs. Season well. Cover, bring back to the boil and continue simmering, keeping the mixture just covered in water, until the meat is tender, about 1½ to 2 hours; long, slow cooking is essential. Serves 6.

Woodpigeon with Mushrooms

Woodpigeons have for long been shot by farmers as an ongoing pest. Although taking some time to cook, their slightly gamy flavour makes a tasty casserole.

4 woodpigeons, prepared
2 oz butter
2 tablespoons oil
2 medium onions, sliced
8 oz mushrooms, halved
1 large cooking apple,
   peeled, cored and sliced

2 tablespoons cranberry jelly
1 bay leaf
¼ pint chicken stock
1 cup cider
1 heaped dessertspoon
   cornflour
Salt and pepper

Heat the butter and oil in a large, flameproof casserole and brown the birds all over. Remove and set aside. Lower the heat and fry the onions until lightly browned. Remove from the heat and add the mushrooms, apple slices, cranberry jelly and bay leaf and season well. Place the pigeons on the mixture and pour over the stock and cider. Bring to the boil, cover and simmer for 2-2½ hours, stirring occasionally. When the pigeons are tender, remove and set aside. Drain off the liquid into a pan, remove the bay leaf and stir in the cornflour, already mixed with a little water. Bring to the boil, stirring until the liquid thickens. Return to the casserole with the pigeons, stir well and finally heat through gently. Serves 4.

Carrot and Potato Soup

Certain foods, like carrots and potatoes, keep well and are a good standby in the galley. In this recipe these two staple vegetables make a tasty, filling soup.

1½ lbs carrots, cut into chunks	**1 clove garlic, crushed**
2 large potatoes, cut into chunks	**1 pint vegetable stock**
2 medium onions, chopped	**¼ pt milk**
1 oz butter	**1 teaspoon medium curry paste**
1 tablespoon oil	**Salt and pepper**

Peel the carrots and potatoes and cut into chunks. Peel and chop the onions and crush the garlic. Heat the butter and oil in a large saucepan, put in the vegetables and stir well. Add the crushed garlic and stock and season well. Bring to the boil, cover and simmer for about 35 minutes or until the vegetables are quite soft. When slightly cooled, rub through a sieve into a clean saucepan, mix in the milk and curry paste, stir well, adjust the seasoning and reheat. Serves 4 to 6.

'Tom Pudding' Pudding

The name of this pudding was inspired by a type of craft used to transport coal in bulk; large, steel box containers known as 'Tom Puddings', joined together in a train with a rounded false bow like half a pudding basin and towed by a powerful tug.

4 oz mixed soft fruits, fresh or frozen   2 large eggs, beaten

first weigh the eggs together and then weigh out the same weight in:
Butter or soft margarine   Caster sugar   Self raising flour

Grease a medium size pudding basin. Cream the butter or margarine and sugar together in a bowl until pale and creamy. Sift in the flour, add the beaten eggs and beat well to a stiffish sponge mixture. If rather thin, beat in a little more flour. Place a layer of the mixture in the bottom of the pudding basin and spread a layer around the sides of the basin, reserving sufficient to make a lid. Fill the centre with the soft fruit mixture and cover with the remaining sponge mixture. Cover and seal with kitchen foil and steam for 1½ hours, topping up the water as necessary. When cooked, run a knife around the basin and turn out on to a serving dish. Serve with custard or cream. Serves 4 to 6.

Chicken and Leek Hobbler

Years ago, when boatmen became old and less active and 'hobbled about', they sought casual work such as helping with locks and moving boats in exchange for a hot meal and a bed. Such men were known as hobblers and this recipe is a salute to them.

6 chicken breasts	**2 medium leeks, chopped**
2 tablespoons wholemeal flour	**2 rashers streaky bacon, chopped**
2 tablespoons porridge oats	**6 oz mushrooms, sliced**
1 tablespoon oil	**2 teaspoons yeast extract**
2 medium onions, sliced	**Salt and pepper**

Set oven to 350°F or Mark 4. Mix the flour and oatmeal together in a large bowl and season well. Coat the chicken breasts evenly with this mixture. Heat the oil in a large flameproof casserole and brown the breasts on both sides. Remove and set aside in the bowl of flour mixture. Re-heat the oil, adding a little extra if necessary, and cook the onions, leeks, bacon and mushrooms, covered, over a medium heat for 5 minutes, stirring to prevent over browning. Replace the breasts with the remaining flour mixture, stir well, add the yeast extract and sufficient water to cover the chicken. Stir, bring to the boil, cover and cook in the oven for about 1½ to 2 hours, until the chicken is tender. Alternatively, simmer on top of the stove for about 1½ hours. Serves 6.

Legging through Shrewley Tunnel, Grand Union Canal

Prawn Bake

Working boaters who transhipped their cargoes near one of the larger seaports could readily buy shrimps. This modern version of an old shrimp recipe works well with prawns.

8 oz small, shelled prawns, fresh or frozen
3 medium eggs, beaten
3-4 oz Cheddar cheese, finely grated

½ pint double cream
Juice of 1 large lemon
Salt and pepper
Sprigs of parsley to garnish

Set oven to 375°F or Mark 5. Wash the prawns and pat dry in a clean teacloth or kitchen paper. Butter 8 ramekin dishes and divide the prawns equally between them. Beat the eggs well in a bowl and stir in the grated cheese and cream and season. Pour the lemon juice equally over each ramekin and then pour over the cream/cheese mixture. Stand the ramekins in a large baking tin containing not less than 1 inch of water and cook in the oven for approximately 20 minutes. Garnish with fresh parsley sprigs and serve as a starter or, with a crisp salad and warm, crusty rolls, as a light lunch or supper dish. Serves 8.

Stewed Pears in Spices

Ripe pears picked off the tree are a real taste of Autumn. This adaptation of an old Worcestershire recipe combines another autumn fruit - blackberries - with the pears. Comice pears are ideal for this dish but are not essential.

6 pears	**¼ - ½ pint sweet cider**
½ lb blackberries	**1 teaspoon dried mixed spice**
¼ - ½ pint red wine	**½ - 1 teaspoon ground ginger**

Wash the blackberries well and peel the pears and leave whole. Put the fruits together into a saucepan, pour on the red wine and add the mixed spice and ground ginger. Gently poach the fruit over a low heat until tender. Remove the pears, cut each one in half, carefully remove the cores and return to the pan. Now just cover with sweet cider, bring to the boil and boil rapidly until the liquid is reduced and syrupy. Serve with whipped cream. Serves 6.

Lamb Stew with Herby Dumplings

Winter was a hard time for working boatmen. Not only were long hours spent standing, steering, in biting winds but locks had to be worked with frozen paddle gear.

3 lbs middle neck of lamb   1 tablespoon sugar   2 dessertspoons flour
3 leeks, chopped   1 small onion, chopped   2 large carrots, cut into chunks
14 oz tin tomatoes   2 cloves garlic, crushed   ¾ pint vegetable stock   1 bay leaf
1 teaspoon dried thyme   2 tablespoons oil   Salt and pepper

DUMPLINGS
8 oz self raising flour   ½ teaspoon salt   4 oz shredded suet   2 teaspoons mixed herbs

Set oven to 350°F or Mark 4. Heat the oil in a large flameproof casserole and quickly brown the meat all over. Sprinkle over the sugar and toss until it caramelises slightly. Season well and stir in half the flour. Cook over a fairly high heat for 5-6 minutes, stirring well. Add the vegetables, tomatoes and garlic, stirring well and then add the remaining flour. Add the stock, bay leaf and thyme and stir. Bring to the boil, cover and simmer on the stove for a few minutes, then put in the oven and cook for 1-1½ hours. Add the dumplings 30 minutes before the end of the cooking time. **Dumplings**. Sift the flour and salt into a basin. Add the herbs and suet and mix thoroughly with only just enough cold water to make a soft dough. Divide the dough into 6-8 dumplings.   Serves 4 to 6.

Pan Fried Trout

Generally speaking, two kinds of trout can be bought these days; the commercially produced rainbow trout and our native brown trout. The latter are more difficult to come by but they have a more delicate flavour.

4 fresh trout, prepared	**4 oz butter**
Seasoned flour	**Salt and pepper**

Wash the fish and pat dry in a clean teacloth or kitchen paper, removing the heads, if preferred. Make 3 diagonal cuts with a sharp knife across both sides of each fish and coat evenly with seasoned flour. Heat half the butter in a frying pan until foaming and brown 2 trout on both sides over a moderate heat. Turn down the heat and continue cooking for about 5 minutes, turning once. Remove from the pan, set aside and keep warm. Heat the rest of the butter and repeat with the other two fish. Serve hot or cold. Serves 4.

Roast Pheasant

In days past many canal boat families kept a dog on board. They acted as watchdogs and, since canalside hedgerows, fields and woods were open to the boatman with his dog and gun, rabbits and game birds were regular additions to the pot.

A brace of young pheasants, prepared	**6 rashers streaky bacon**
A little seasoned flour	**Salt and pepper**
2 oz butter	**2 slices wholemeal toast**

Set oven to 425°F or Mark 7. Wipe the birds with kitchen paper and check for and remove any stray feathers and shot. Sprinkle the inside of each bird with seasoned flour and place a good knob of butter inside each one to keep them moist during cooking. Spread the remaining butter on the breasts and legs, season and lay the rashers of bacon over the birds. Place each bird on a piece of toast in a roasting tin and put in the oven. Allow 20 minutes per pound cooking time. Baste frequently during cooking and remove the bacon rashers for the last 10-15 minutes to brown the skin. Serve with mashed potatoes, Brussels sprouts or peas and bread sauce. Serves 4.

Leeks in Cheese Sauce

A good, tasty cheese is the basis for this dish; strong Cheddar or Lancashire or Cheshire work well. Leeks are a versatile vegetable, milder than onions, yet flavoursome in soups and casseroles and in simple lunch or supper dishes, as this old favourite.

4-6 large leeks, sliced	**2 oz flour**
6-8 oz strong, hard cheese	**¾-1 pint milk**
eg. grated	**1 bay leaf**
2-3 oz butter	**Salt and pepper**

Set oven to 400°F or Mark 6. Wash the leeks well and cut into thick slices. Parboil the leeks for 8-10 minutes, drain well and put in a buttered, ovenproof dish. Heat the milk in a saucepan with the bay leaf then set aside and allow to stand, covered, for 10 minutes then remove the bay leaf. Grate the cheese finely. Melt the butter in a pan, remove from the heat, stir in the flour and beat well. Slowly add the milk, mixing well and beat again. Return the pan to the heat and stir until the sauce boils and thickens. Again remove the pan from the heat and beat in the grated cheese. Pour the sauce over the leeks, put in the oven and cook until golden brown on top. Serves 4 to 6.

Beef in Beer

One of the joys of chugging along a canal or river is the discovery of a hitherto unvisited waterside pub. Real ales vary considerably in different parts of the country; this recipe calls for a hearty bitter or a brown ale, not a lager.

2 lbs lean stewing steak	**1 cup beer**
Seasoned flour	**¼-½ pint water**
2 medium onions, sliced	**4 large potatoes, sliced**
1 tablespoon tomato purée	**Salt and pepper**
Pinch of dried mixed herbs	**Oil for frying**

Cut the meat into 1 inch cubes and toss in seasoned flour. Heat 2 tablespoons of oil in a large, flameproof casserole and brown the meat all over. Remove and set aside. Add a little more oil if necessary and gently fry the onions until soft but not brown. Turn down the heat, replace the meat, add the tomato purée, herbs, beer and any remaining flour and add sufficient water just to cover. Place the sliced potatoes in a layer over the meat and season well. Bring to the boil, cover and simmer gently for about 2 hours until the meat is tender and the potato layer is soft. Add more boiling water during cooking if required. Serves 4.

Bubble and Squeak

Traditionally served on a Monday, to use up left-over cooked vegetables from Sunday lunch with the cold meat, Bubble and Squeak also makes a good, quick meal on its own and is especially useful when the boat is under way and the cook is being kept busy.

1 lb cooked potatoes, mashed	**1 medium onion, finely chopped**
8 oz cooked cabbage or	**4 tablespoons butter or oil**
Brussels sprouts	**Salt and pepper**

Heat half the butter or oil in a heavy frying pan. Add the onion and cook gently, stirring frequently, until softened but not browned. Mix together the onion, the mashed potatoes and the cooked greens and season well. Put the vegetable mixture into the pan and press down with a slice into a thick even cake. Fry over a moderate heat for 10 to 15 minutes until the underside is browned. Hold a large plate over the cake and invert the pan to transfer the cake on to the plate. Add the remaining butter or oil to the pan and re-heat. When hot, slip the cake off the plate back into the pan and fry, as before, until the second side is browned. Cut into wedges and serve. Serves 4.

At Fradley Junction, Trent and Mersey Canal

Alan Firth

Navvy's Stew

*This dish is a tribute to all the gangs of hard working navvies who dug
the canals in the 18th and 19th centuries. The conditions under
which they worked were harsh and often dangerous.*

2 lbs best end of neck of lamb
Seasoned flour
2 medium onions, chopped
4 medium carrots, sliced
Good bunch of parsley, chopped
¼ teaspoon English mustard

Large sprig of fresh thyme or
   1-2 teaspoons dried thyme
½-¾ pint Guinness
½ pint vegetable stock
Oil for frying
Salt and pepper

Trim the meat and coat in seasoned flour. Heat 2 tablespoons oil in a large
flameproof casserole and brown the meat all over. Remove and set aside. Add
another tablespoon of oil and fry the onions and carrots until soft but not brown.
Replace the meat and add the parsley, thyme, mustard and any surplus flour. Pour
in the Guinness and the stock, stir well and season. Bring to the boil, cover, turn
down the heat and simmer slowly for 1½ to 2 hours until the meat is tender. Add
more boiling water if required during cooking. Serves 4.

Wychnor Lock Pudding

The author Tom Rolt was renowned for his voyaging in his narrowboat Cressy. In his famous book 'Narrow Boat' he tells of going through Wychnor Lock on the Trent and Mersey Canal and being given "a fine basket of blackberries" by the lock-keeper.

8 oz blackberries **3 oz sugar (or more if preferred)**
1 tablespoon water **2 egg whites**
6 fl.oz double cream

Wash the blackberries and put into a saucepan with the tablespoon of water. Bring to the boil and simmer gently until the fruit is cooked. Cool and rub through a sieve. Stir the sugar into the fruit purée. Whip the egg whites until they form soft peaks and whip the cream until it just holds its shape. Combine the egg white and cream and then fold in the fruit purée and stir to blend. Pour into a serving bowl and decorate with a few blackberries. Serves 4 to 6. It is inadvisable to serve uncooked egg whites to young children or very elderly people.

Wild Duck with Apples

Wild duck formed part of the old boatmen's diet but are less easy to come by today. When obtainable they have a distinctive flavour, but a domestic bird can be used instead.

2 wild ducks or 1 duck approx. 5 lbs, prepared   3 oz butter   1 tablespoon oil
3 tablespoons brandy   ¼ pint white wine   ½ pint chicken stock
Juice of ½ orange   Salt and pepper
APPLE SAUCE
1 lb cooking apples, peeled, cored and sliced   4 tablespoons cider or water
2-3 tablespoons sugar   2 tablespoons butter   Pinch of cinnamon (if desired)

Set oven to 325°F or Mark 3. Wipe the bird(s) inside and out and rub the skin with salt and freshly ground pepper. Heat the butter and oil in a large flameproof casserole and brown the duck(s) all over. Warm the brandy, pour over the duck(s) and set aflame. Next, pour over the wine and stock, bring to the boil, cover and cook in the oven for 1½-2 hours. When cooked, transfer the duck(s) to a serving dish and keep hot. Meanwhile, strain the cooking juices into a bowl, spoon off the fat and return to the casserole. Add the apple sauce and orange juice, heat through and stir well. Pour over the duck(s) and serve with boiled potatoes and a green vegetable. Serves 4. **Apple sauce.** Simmer the apples in a saucepan with the cider or water until soft, add the sugar and butter and cinnamon (if desired) and beat well.

METRIC CONVERSIONS

The weights, measures and oven temperatures used in the preceding recipes can be easily converted to their metric equivalents. The conversions listed below are only approximate, having been rounded up or down as may be appropriate.

Weights

Avoirdupois	Metric
1 oz.	just under 30 grams
4 oz. (¼ lb.)	app. 115 grams
8 oz. (½ lb.)	app. 230 grams
1 lb.	454 grams

Liquid Measures

Imperial	Metric
1 tablespoon (liquid only)	20 millilitres
1 fl. oz.	app. 30 millilitres
1 gill (¼ pt.)	app. 145 millilitres
½ pt.	app. 285 millilitres
1 pt.	app. 570 millilitres
1 qt.	app. 1.140 litres

Oven Temperatures

	°Fahrenheit	Gas Mark	°Celsius
Slow	300	2	150
	325	3	170
Moderate	350	4	180
	375	5	190
	400	6	200
Hot	425	7	220
	450	8	230
	475	9	240

Flour as specified in these recipes refers to Plain Flour unless otherwise described.